© 2024 RP Macleod. All rights reserved.

No part of this book may be reproduced, distributed, or transmitted in any form or by any means, including photocopying, recording, or other electronic or mechanical methods, without the prior written permission of the author, except in the case of brief quotations embodied in critical reviews or articles.

This book is a work of research and analysis. The views expressed are those of the author and do not necessarily reflect the views of any organizations mentioned. The information presented in this book is accurate to the best of the author's knowledge at the time of publication.

Contents

1 The Global Origins of Sovereignty Movements

2 Core Beliefs and Misconceptions

3 The Appeal and Psychology Behind the Movement

4 Tax Resistance Laws Around the World

5 Courtroom Battles Across Borders

6 Personal and Societal Costs of Tax Resistance

7 Risks of Pseudolegal Beliefs in a Global Context

8 Debunking Global Freemen Myths

9 Rebuilding Trust and Advocacy Worldwide

Conclusion A Universal Call for Critical Thinking

Authors Note

When I first set out to research the topic of freemen movements and the ideologies that fuel them, I had no idea just how much information I would uncover. The deeper I delved, the more I realized how pervasive these beliefs have become, particularly in the vast reaches of social media. What began as a curiosity quickly turned into a mission to understand not only the origins of these movements, but also the psychology behind them and the global impact they have had on individuals and societies. In a world where misinformation spreads at lightning speed, the allure of these ideas can be tempting, and the desire to escape the complexities of the legal system can feel overwhelmingly strong.

Throughout my research, I encountered a range of perspectives, from those fervently advocating for the sovereignty movement to those who had suffered severe consequences after falling prey to its pseudolegal arguments. The constant across these stories was the overwhelming presence of social media as both a breeding ground and an amplifier for these beliefs. Online forums, blogs, and social media platforms have allowed these ideologies to spread rapidly, often without scrutiny or factual correction, leaving many individuals vulnerable to their seductive promises of easy solutions to complex issues.

As I navigated through this subject, I made it my mission to approach it with an open mind and an unwavering commitment to presenting the facts. It was important to me that this book not become just another opinion piece or an attack on those who subscribe to these ideologies. Instead, I wanted to create a resource that laid out the reality of the freemen movement: its history, its core beliefs, the consequences of embracing it, and the broader societal implications. This book is the result of many hours of research, reflection, and a genuine desire to shed light on the facts, to demystify the myths, and to provide a resource for anyone seeking to understand this complex issue.

I hope that, in reading this, you are able to take away not only a clearer understanding of the global freemen movement, but also the tools to recognize misinformation and to approach any legal, political, or social issue with a critical and informed mind. Ultimately, the goal is to empower readers to make better decisions and to encourage dialogue that leads to positive change—not just within legal systems, but in the broader context of building trust, accountability, and informed action in our societies.

Thank you for taking the time to explore this important topic with me. I encourage you to remain curious, to question what you encounter, and, most importantly, to always seek the truth.

1 The Global Origins of Sovereignty Movements

1 The Global Origins of Sovereignty Movements

The idea of sovereignty has captivated individuals across generations, drawing from the universal desire for freedom and self-determination. At its core, sovereignty signifies the ability to exist independently, free from interference or control by external forces. This concept, while appearing straightforward, is steeped in complexity, shaped by centuries of historical evolution and adapted by various movements around the globe. To truly understand the modern interpretations of sovereignty, we must delve into its global origins and explore how individuals in different cultures and societies have pursued their own paths to independence.

Sovereignty's roots stretch far back into ancient history, emerging in societies where power was consolidated in the hands of a few. From kings and emperors to feudal lords, the rulers of ancient civilizations often exercised near-total control over their subjects, dictating every aspect of life. Yet, even in these rigid hierarchies, whispers of rebellion and autonomy began to take hold. In ancient

Greece, for example, the seeds of democracy were planted, offering citizens an unprecedented voice in governance. This was a radical shift, a moment when people began to imagine the possibility of self-rule rather than submission to authority.

The Enlightenment era in Europe further ignited the flames of sovereignty. Philosophers such as John Locke, Jean-Jacques Rousseau, and Immanuel Kant articulated ideas about natural rights, individual freedoms, and the social contract. These thinkers challenged the status quo, arguing that authority should derive from the consent of the governed. Their writings inspired revolutions, transforming the intellectual landscape and laying the groundwork for movements that sought to claim independence from oppressive systems.

The American Revolution stands as a defining moment in the history of sovereignty. Colonists in the New World, fed up with taxation without representation and other perceived injustices, declared their independence from British rule. This act of defiance was not only a declaration of political separation but also a statement of belief in the right to self-governance. The principles enshrined in the Declaration of Independence and later in the U.S. Constitution became a beacon for those seeking autonomy worldwide. Over time, these ideals were adapted and reinterpreted by movements in other nations, particularly in the context of personal sovereignty.

Across the Atlantic, the United Kingdom experienced its own sovereignty debates, albeit in a different form. The British monarchy, long the symbol of centralized power, gradually ceded authority to a parliamentary system. Even as these shifts occurred, movements emerged that rejected the authority of both the monarchy and the government. By the late 20th century, a group identifying as "freemen on the land" began asserting their right to live outside of state-imposed legal and financial obligations. These individuals claimed that by invoking certain common law principles, they could effectively opt out of paying taxes or following government regulations. Their interpretations of the law were often flawed, but their persistence reflected a broader dissatisfaction with the existing system.

In Canada, sovereignty movements followed a similar trajectory, influenced by the country's shared legal heritage with Britain. The "freeman-on-the-land" ideology gained traction in the early 2000s, with adherents claiming they could sever ties with the government through specific legal declarations. These claims rested on the belief that the government operated as a corporate entity, binding individuals into contracts they could refuse. While these arguments lacked legal validity, they resonated with those who felt alienated from the system, offering a sense of empowerment even in the face of widespread criticism.

Australia and New Zealand have also seen the rise of sovereignty movements, many of which borrowed ideas from their North American and British counterparts. These groups often argue that their constitutional frameworks grant them the right to reject taxes, licenses, and other obligations imposed by the state. In some cases, these movements have even tied their arguments to indigenous land rights disputes, attempting to blend historical grievances with contemporary sovereignty claims. This blending of legal theories and historical injustices has created a uniquely complex landscape in these countries.

Europe presents yet another variation of sovereignty ideologies, shaped by its diverse legal and cultural traditions. In Germany, for instance, sovereign citizen movements have emerged under different names, often linking their beliefs to conspiracy theories about globalization and government control. In Eastern Europe, where distrust in government institutions has long been prevalent, sovereignty claims have found fertile ground, particularly among those who view the state as corrupt or illegitimate. These movements frequently adapt their arguments to align with local circumstances, using regional history and law to bolster their claims.

One of the most significant developments in the global spread of sovereignty ideologies has been the rise of the internet. In the digital age, ideas that once remained localized can now cross borders with ease. Sovereignty movements have capitalized on this, sharing strategies and legal theories across countries. For example, the "strawman" theory, which posits that governments create a fictitious legal entity for each person, has its roots in the United States but has since been adopted by groups in Canada, the U.K., Australia, and beyond. This theory claims that by rejecting the strawman identity, individuals can reclaim their sovereignty—a notion that has been consistently debunked but remains popular among adherents.

The adaptability of sovereignty movements is one of their defining characteristics. While the core principles—rejecting taxes, licenses, and government authority—remain consistent, the arguments used to justify these positions often reflect the legal and cultural nuances of specific regions. In common law countries like the U.S., U.K., and Canada, references to constitutional rights and historical legal traditions are common. In civil law countries, arguments may focus more on perceived loopholes in statutory codes. This ability to tailor their message has allowed sovereignty movements to gain traction in diverse contexts, even as they face legal and social challenges.

Despite their variations, sovereignty movements share certain vulnerabilities, particularly their reliance on pseudolegal arguments that fail to hold up in court. From tax evasion cases to disputes over property rights, the outcomes are nearly always the same: the courts reaffirm the authority of the state, and the individuals involved face legal consequences. Yet, the persistence of these movements suggests that they tap into a deeper dissatisfaction with modern governance. For many, sovereignty ideologies offer a sense of agency in a world that often feels overwhelming and impersonal.

Understanding the global origins of sovereignty movements allows us to see beyond their surface-level claims. At their heart, these movements reflect a universal desire for autonomy and control, particularly in times of economic or political uncertainty. They also highlight the challenges of navigating complex legal systems, which can leave individuals feeling powerless or alienated. While the arguments of freemen and similar groups may lack legal foundation, their enduring appeal underscores the importance of addressing the underlying concerns that drive people to embrace such ideologies.

The story of sovereignty movements is not merely about legal disputes or tax resistance. It is a story about the human quest for freedom, the limits of authority, and the power of ideas to inspire and mislead. By examining their global origins, we can better understand the factors that sustain these movements and find ways to address the needs they claim to fulfill. In doing so, we can promote a more informed and equitable dialogue about freedom, responsibility, and the role of governance in our lives.

2 Core Beliefs and Misconceptions

2 Core Beliefs and Misconceptions

Sovereignty movements, especially those associated with the freeman-on-the-land ideology, share a set of core beliefs that transcend national boundaries. These beliefs resonate deeply with individuals who feel alienated or frustrated with the governing systems of their countries. Though the specific legal and philosophical foundations of these movements vary by region, there are consistent themes that underpin them, such as rejecting taxation, opposing government authority, and embracing pseudolegal arguments. These movements often present themselves as alternatives to the established legal and governmental structures, suggesting that individuals can reclaim control over their own lives and circumvent what they see as unjust systems.

One of the most central and persistent ideas in these movements is the rejection of taxation. For many adherents, taxes represent an unjust appropriation of their income by the government. The belief is rooted in a fundamental distrust of the state's role in economic and social affairs. Supporters argue that taxation is a form of coercion, an infringement on personal sovereignty, and that individuals should have the right to decide how their wealth is allocated. The desire to avoid paying taxes leads many to believe they can opt out of the system entirely, claiming that they can avoid taxes through legal loopholes or by asserting their sovereignty over the government.

This rejection of taxation is often accompanied by a deep mistrust of government institutions. Freemen and others who subscribe to similar ideologies view the state as a coercive and illegitimate entity. The government is seen not as a service provider but as an adversary that seeks to impose control over individuals' lives. This distrust is frequently fueled by a sense of disillusionment with the political system, particularly in countries where corruption, inefficiency, or political polarization have eroded public faith in elected officials. For those who believe in personal sovereignty, the idea of being subject to government rules, regulations, and taxes is not just an inconvenience, but an infringement on their basic rights as free individuals.

At the heart of many sovereignty movements lies the use of pseudolegal arguments. These arguments, often rooted in conspiracy theories or misinterpretations of legal principles, are intended to provide adherents with a framework for rejecting government authority.

One of the most common legal myths propagated by freemen is the idea that governments create a "strawman" for every citizen. According to this theory, individuals are not the living, breathing persons they perceive themselves to be, but rather corporate entities created by the government for legal and financial purposes. By rejecting this "strawman" identity, individuals believe they can free themselves from legal obligations such as paying taxes or following laws. However, this idea is entirely unsupported by legal precedent, and courts consistently reject it.

Another widely circulated legal myth in freeman circles is the belief in the primacy of maritime law. In many commonwealth countries, particularly in the United Kingdom, Australia, and Canada, there is a persistent misconception that the legal system is based on maritime or admiralty law. According to this belief, because maritime law supposedly governs commercial transactions, all laws are part of a corporate system that can be circumvented. Proponents of this idea argue that by declaring themselves outside of maritime law, they can reclaim their sovereignty. However, this claim is similarly without merit, as the legal systems in these countries are based on centuries of common law and statutory law, not maritime law.

These misconceptions often evolve in response to specific regional issues, creating distinctive ideologies in different parts of the world. For example, in the United States, the idea of "constitutional sovereignty" is frequently invoked, where individuals claim that by invoking certain clauses of the Constitution, they can opt out of federal jurisdiction and control. In the United Kingdom, the focus may be on common law, with freemen asserting that they are not subject to government-imposed laws and taxes. In Canada and Australia, the arguments often blend elements of constitutional law with maritime law theories, resulting in a patchwork of legal myths that vary in sophistication but share the same fundamental rejection of state authority.

These regional differences in freemen ideologies demonstrate how local legal traditions, histories, and social contexts shape the specific beliefs and strategies of sovereignty movements. However, despite these variations, the core themes—rejection of taxation, mistrust of government, and reliance on pseudolegal arguments—remain constant. These ideologies offer individuals a sense of empowerment, providing an alternative narrative that allows them to resist perceived oppression and claim control over their lives.

The rise of social media and online forums has played a crucial role in the spread of these beliefs across borders. In the past, sovereignty movements were largely confined to specific countries or regions, but the internet has allowed these ideas to circulate globally. Online communities dedicated to freemen ideologies have created networks that facilitate the sharing of legal theories, strategies for avoiding taxes, and personal success stories. Social media platforms, discussion forums, and YouTube videos have become essential tools for propagating the core beliefs of these movements, allowing individuals to connect with like-minded people from around the world.

These online spaces also foster a sense of solidarity among adherents, as individuals are able to exchange information and offer support to one another. The spread of legal myths is amplified through these platforms, as individuals share documents, videos, and personal testimonies that reinforce the belief in personal sovereignty. Online influencers, some of whom claim to be "sovereign experts," often provide advice on how to navigate legal systems and avoid government intervention. While these influencers may not be legally qualified, their message resonates with people who are looking for alternatives to the traditional systems of power and control.

The proliferation of social media has made it easier for sovereignty movements to gain visibility, but it has also led to the amplification of misinformation. Pseudolegal arguments and debunked legal theories are frequently presented as truth, often without any counter arguments or fact-checking. For many individuals, the appeal of the movement lies not in the legal soundness of its arguments but in the sense of empowerment and control it offers. The promise of freedom from taxes, government regulations, and legal obligations can be enticing, particularly for those who feel disillusioned by the system they live under.

However, the spread of these ideas also has significant consequences. Individuals who attempt to apply pseudolegal arguments in real life often face legal challenges, including fines, lawsuits, and criminal charges. The courts consistently reject the claims made by freemen and similar groups, reinforcing the authority of the government and the legal system. Yet, despite these setbacks, the appeal of sovereignty movements remains strong, as many individuals continue to seek alternative ways of navigating the complex systems of law and governance that they feel trapped within.

The global spread of freemen ideologies underscores the power of ideas in shaping individual behavior and influencing social movements. The desire for personal sovereignty and autonomy is a deeply ingrained human instinct, one that transcends borders and cultures. While the legal myths and pseudolegal arguments espoused by these movements may be flawed, they tap into a larger dissatisfaction with the current state of governance, law, and societal structures. As these movements continue to evolve, it is essential to understand the core beliefs and misconceptions that drive them, as well as the ways in which they spread and gain traction worldwide.

3 The Appeal and Psychology Behind the Movement

3 The Appeal and Psychology Behind the Movement

The sovereignty movement has captured the imaginations of individuals across the globe, drawing people from various backgrounds, cultures, and socio-economic classes. What is it about this ideology that resonates so deeply with people from such different walks of life? To understand the appeal of sovereignty movements, we must explore the psychological and societal factors that drive individuals to adopt these beliefs. These ideologies are not merely intellectual pursuits; they are born from real-life frustrations and concerns that many individuals feel on a personal level. The appeal of the freeman-on-the-land movement and similar ideologies lies in the promise of self-empowerment and autonomy, offering an alternative narrative for those who feel oppressed, disenfranchised, or powerless in a complex, bureaucratic world.

One of the key factors driving people towards sovereignty movements is economic disparity. As wealth inequality continues to grow, many individuals feel the pinch of economic hardship, whether through stagnant wages, rising living costs, or the erosion of job security. This sense of economic injustice can lead people to question the fairness of the system they live under. Sovereignty ideologies often target these grievances by promoting the idea that individuals can break free from the systems that they believe are causing their economic struggles. They suggest that by rejecting government authority, taxes, and the obligations of the traditional financial system, one can gain control over their own wealth and resources. The promise of financial freedom and independence is incredibly enticing for those who feel trapped by a system that seems designed to benefit the wealthy while leaving the rest behind.

Economic disparity is not the only force driving people towards sovereignty movements. Distrust in institutions is another major factor that plays a significant role. In many parts of the world, people have grown disillusioned with the traditional institutions of government, law, and politics. This distrust is often fueled by corruption, inefficiency, and perceived injustice. Governments are frequently seen as out of touch with the needs of the people, making decisions that benefit a select few while ignoring the struggles of the masses. This sense of alienation can make sovereignty ideologies, with their anti-government and anti-establishment rhetoric, feel like a natural solution. When individuals believe that the very systems meant to protect and serve them are instead perpetuating inequality and injustice, rejecting those systems can seem like a powerful act of resistance.

Moreover, the global rise of anti-globalization sentiments has also contributed to the spread of sovereignty movements. As the world becomes increasingly interconnected, many people feel that their local cultures, economies, and identities are being eroded by global forces. Economic globalization, mass migration, and the spread of multinational corporations have created a sense of loss of control over local affairs. This has led to a growing backlash against global institutions, including the United Nations, the World Bank, and international trade agreements. In this context, sovereignty ideologies provide a way for people to reclaim what they feel has been taken from them—control over their own land, laws, and resources. The idea of returning to a more localized, self-determined way of life holds great appeal for those who feel marginalized by the globalized world.

In addition to economic factors and distrust in institutions, the psychology of conspiracy theories plays a central role in the allure of sovereignty movements. Conspiracy theories offer simple explanations for complex societal issues, making them particularly attractive during times of uncertainty and upheaval. Many adherents of sovereignty ideologies believe that the government and the legal system are part of a larger conspiracy to control and manipulate the population. These theories often paint a picture of a world where powerful elites operate in the shadows, pulling the strings of governments and corporations for their own benefit. For individuals who feel powerless or oppressed, these conspiracies provide a framework for understanding the world and a sense of purpose in fighting against these hidden forces.

One of the most prominent conspiracy theories within the sovereignty movement is the idea that governments create "strawman" identities for their citizens, which can then be used to extract taxes, impose laws, and control individuals. According to this belief, the government creates a legal fiction for each person that exists separately from their true self, and by rejecting or disavowing this "strawman," individuals can free themselves from legal obligations. While this idea has been thoroughly debunked in legal circles, it continues to appeal to those who are drawn to the idea of breaking free from what they perceive as a rigged system.

Social media and the internet have played a critical role in the spread of these conspiracy theories and in shaping the psychology of the sovereignty movement. Online platforms provide a space for people to share their beliefs and connect with others who hold similar views. Social media has created a global community of freemen and sovereign citizens who can exchange ideas, strategies, and success stories. This sense of belonging to a like-minded group can be highly empowering for individuals who feel isolated or marginalized in their offline lives. Social media amplifies the voices of these movements, providing a platform for their ideologies to reach a global audience. At the same time, it can also reinforce existing beliefs by creating echo chambers, where individuals are only exposed to information that confirms their pre-existing views. This phenomenon, known as the "filter bubble," has made it easier for conspiracy theories to spread unchecked and for individuals to become more entrenched in their beliefs.

Furthermore, the role of influencers and self-proclaimed experts has been pivotal in legitimizing these beliefs for followers. Many individuals within the sovereignty movement turn to these influencers for guidance, believing that they have uncovered hidden truths that the mainstream media and legal systems are deliberately concealing. These influencers often present themselves as knowledgeable and experienced, offering advice on how to navigate legal systems, avoid taxes, and assert one's sovereignty. Some even sell courses, books, or consulting services that promise to help individuals "break free" from government control. Despite the fact that many of these so-called experts have little to no formal legal training, they manage to gain large followings by presenting their ideas in an authoritative and convincing manner.

The appeal of sovereignty ideologies also lies in their ability to offer a sense of control and empowerment. For people who feel powerless or overwhelmed by the complexities of modern life, the idea that they can opt out of the system and take control of their own destiny is incredibly appealing. These ideologies promise a way to escape from the burdens of taxes, legal obligations, and government interference, allowing individuals to live life on their own terms. The idea of reclaiming personal sovereignty resonates with the universal desire for freedom and autonomy, making it a powerful motivator for those who feel disillusioned by the structures of power that govern their lives.

In conclusion, the psychology behind the appeal of sovereignty ideologies is complex and multifaceted. Economic disparity, distrust in institutions, anti-globalization sentiments, and conspiracy theories all play significant roles in driving individuals towards these beliefs. The rise of social media has further amplified these movements, providing a platform for them to spread globally. While the promises of sovereignty ideologies may be alluring, the reality is often much more complicated. Nevertheless, understanding the psychological and societal factors that drive these movements is essential to addressing the issues that fuel their growth and to helping individuals who may feel lost or disillusioned find more constructive ways to engage with society and its institutions.

4 Tax Resistance Laws Around the World

4 Tax Resistance Laws Around the World

The idea of resisting taxation is central to many sovereignty movements, and it is perhaps one of the most contentious issues they address. Across the globe, the question of who should pay taxes, how much, and under what circumstances is an ongoing debate. Many freemen and sovereignty movements reject the idea of taxation, often arguing that the government has no legal or moral right to take money from individuals. While these movements may share similar beliefs, the systems of taxation in various countries are diverse, and understanding how tax resistance plays out globally requires an exploration of these different tax structures and how they are challenged by those who resist them.

The taxation systems around the world differ significantly in their structure, philosophy, and execution. In most modern countries, taxes are a critical source of revenue for governments, used to fund essential services like healthcare, education, infrastructure, and social welfare programs. However, the methods by which governments collect taxes and the rates at which they tax can vary greatly. In some countries, tax systems are progressive, meaning that the wealthier individuals pay a higher percentage of their income in taxes. In others, there may be flat taxes or regressive tax systems where the tax burden is heavier on those with lower incomes.

One of the central principles behind most tax systems is the notion of collective responsibility. Governments argue that taxes are essential to maintaining and improving society as a whole, and that everyone, regardless of income, has a responsibility to contribute. However, this idea of collective responsibility is not always accepted by individuals, especially those in sovereignty movements. Many freemen reject the legitimacy of the government's claim to their income, arguing that taxation is a form of theft. They believe that the government has no moral or legal authority to take their money and that they should have the right to choose how their wealth is distributed. This belief is deeply rooted in the idea of personal sovereignty, where individuals see themselves as free from government control and interference.

Freemen who advocate for tax resistance often argue that there is no valid legal basis for taxation. They may claim that the government's ability to tax is derived from a "strawman" identity or that taxation is only applicable to citizens who voluntarily consent to it. Some even argue that the government's legal framework is based on fraudulent or illegitimate laws, and therefore, they are not bound by them. However, these arguments, though popular within the sovereignty movement, fail to hold up in court. Legal experts consistently reject these claims, and courts around the world have repeatedly upheld the legality of tax systems, regardless of the pseudolegal arguments put forth by freemen.

Despite these legal setbacks, tax resistance movements continue to proliferate globally. In many countries, there are groups of individuals who have attempted to refuse to pay taxes, often citing similar reasons to those espoused by freemen. These movements can range from small, local groups to larger, more organized campaigns. While the specific reasons for resistance vary from place to place, the central theme of challenging government authority and rejecting taxes as an unjust form of control remains consistent.

In the United States, for example, there is a long history of tax resistance. One of the most well-known examples is the "tax protester" movement, which has been active for decades. Tax protesters often argue that the federal income tax is unconstitutional, citing various interpretations of the Constitution and legal theories to support their claims. Some have attempted to use the "strawman" theory, while others argue that the federal government has no authority to impose income taxes on individuals. Despite these arguments, tax resisters in the U.S. have faced legal consequences, including fines, penalties, and even imprisonment. The IRS has been highly effective in pursuing individuals who refuse to pay taxes, and courts consistently uphold the legality of the federal income tax.

In Canada, a similar tax resistance movement has emerged, though it operates under different legal frameworks. Canadian tax resisters often argue that the tax system is unjust, claiming that taxes are a form of theft or that they are not legally obligated to pay because they are not "subject" to Canadian law. The Canadian government has responded to these claims with robust legal enforcement, and individuals who refuse to pay taxes often face significant penalties. In one notable case, a group of Canadian tax resisters attempted to use the "sovereign citizen" defense in court, but their arguments were rejected, and they were held accountable for their tax obligations. Like their counterparts in the United States, Canadian tax resisters have learned the hard way that rejecting taxes does not exempt them from the law.

Australia, too, has seen its own tax resistance movements, with some individuals refusing to pay taxes based on similar pseudolegal arguments. Freemen in Australia often argue that they are not subject to the country's tax laws, invoking theories such as the belief in "common law" or the idea that they are not citizens of the country but rather free individuals who are not bound by the rules of the government. The Australian Tax Office (ATO) has aggressively pursued tax resisters, and those who refuse to comply with the nation's tax laws have faced significant legal and financial consequences. The government has made it clear that these arguments hold no legal weight, and the courts have consistently ruled in favor of the ATO's right to enforce tax collection.

In the United Kingdom, tax resistance has also gained traction among freemen and sovereign citizens, although these movements are less widespread than in the U.S. or Canada. UK tax resisters often invoke similar legal theories, arguing that the government has no right to impose taxes or that they are not subject to the country's laws. The UK tax authority, Her Majesty's Revenue and Customs (HMRC), has responded firmly, asserting that tax resistance is unlawful and that individuals who refuse to pay taxes are subject to legal penalties. UK courts have consistently upheld the legitimacy of the country's tax laws, rejecting the arguments put forward by freemen.

Tax resistance movements are not limited to Western countries. In countries around the world, individuals have sought to challenge taxation systems, often in response to economic hardship or political dissatisfaction. In some cases, these movements have gained significant traction, while in others, they remain on the fringes of society. Regardless of the country, however, the legal reality remains the same: governments have the authority to collect taxes, and those who refuse to pay will face legal consequences.

One of the most interesting aspects of tax resistance movements globally is the way in which they share common themes, despite the legal differences between countries. The rejection of government authority, the belief in personal sovereignty, and the desire to escape financial obligations are universal motivations for those who resist taxes. However, these movements tend to fail when they encounter the legal systems of their respective countries. Governments around the world are equipped with the legal tools to enforce tax collection, and courts are generally unwilling to entertain the pseudolegal arguments put forth by tax resisters. Despite the setbacks faced by these movements, the underlying beliefs in sovereignty and individual freedom continue to resonate with people who feel disenfranchised by the state.

In conclusion, tax resistance movements around the world are driven by similar psychological and philosophical beliefs, yet the legal and practical outcomes are often the same. Whether in the United States, Canada, Australia, the United Kingdom, or elsewhere, individuals who resist taxes based on the principles of sovereignty often find themselves facing legal challenges and penalties. The global similarities in freemen arguments underscore the widespread desire for personal freedom and control over one's financial destiny. However, the legal realities of taxation are clear: governments have the authority to collect taxes, and resistance to those taxes will ultimately lead to legal and financial consequences. As sovereignty movements continue to evolve, it is clear that the battle between individual freedom and state authority will remain a central issue in the ongoing debate about the role of government in society.

5 Courtroom Battles Across Borders

5 Courtroom Battles Across Borders

Freemen-like ideologies, though rooted in the rejection of government authority, often clash head-on with established legal systems. In different countries, individuals who align with sovereignty movements frequently find themselves in legal battles where their arguments about tax resistance, personal sovereignty, and rejection of government control are put to the test. The courtroom, however, is not a place where these ideologies often find success. Across the United States, the United Kingdom, Canada, Australia, and beyond, the legal systems have consistently ruled against the claims put forward by those who argue they are exempt from taxes or laws due to their beliefs in personal sovereignty. The legal landscape surrounding these movements offers insights into how governments and courts respond to these challenges, providing a clearer understanding of the complex relationship between freemen and the law.

In the United States, one of the most notable legal battles involving freemen-like ideologies revolves around the so-called "tax protester" movement. This movement, which has been active for decades, has seen individuals challenge the legality of the federal income tax. A central argument of tax protesters is that the federal government's taxation system is unconstitutional or that individuals are not required to pay taxes unless they voluntarily agree to do so. This argument is often rooted in a belief that the U.S. government does not have the constitutional authority to tax citizens, or that citizens can opt-out of tax obligations based on pseudolegal theories such as the "strawman" identity.

One of the most infamous cases in the U.S. related to freemen ideologies is that of Irwin Schiff, a prominent tax protester who spent much of his life challenging the legitimacy of the income tax system. Schiff argued that the federal income tax was unconstitutional and that individuals were not obligated to pay it unless they were engaged in certain activities, such as working for the federal government. His writings and public speeches contributed to the spread of these beliefs, but in the end, Schiff was convicted of tax evasion and sentenced to prison. His case is a powerful reminder of how the U.S. legal system has consistently upheld the constitutionality of income taxes. Courts have repeatedly rejected the claims made by tax protesters and freemen-like individuals, and they have found that refusing to pay taxes based on these beliefs is not a valid legal defense.

In Canada, the legal landscape surrounding freemen-like ideologies is similarly unyielding. Canadian tax resisters often argue that they are not subject to the country's tax laws or that they are free from the legal framework imposed by the Canadian government. These arguments typically involve the belief that the individual has not consented to the authority of the state or that they are not "subjects" of Canadian law. One of the most prominent cases in Canada involving these beliefs is that of the "Sovereign Citizen" movement, which is closely aligned with freemen ideologies. Members of this movement have sought to challenge Canadian tax laws, using legal theories that claim tax obligations do not apply to them.

One of the most publicized legal battles in Canada involved the case of the "Freedom Fighters," a group of individuals who attempted to challenge Canada's tax laws by refusing to file tax returns and pay taxes. The Canadian government responded with legal action, and the courts found the arguments presented by the tax resistors to be without merit. The legal system in Canada firmly rejected the idea that individuals could simply opt out of paying taxes based on personal beliefs, and individuals who refused to comply with tax laws faced serious consequences, including large fines and imprisonment. Just as in the United States, the Canadian legal system reaffirmed that individuals are legally obligated to pay taxes and that rejecting this obligation does not absolve them from legal consequences.

In the United Kingdom, tax resistance movements that share similarities with freemen ideologies have also faced significant legal challenges. The most notable of these challenges occurred in the early 2000s, when a group of individuals who identified as "sovereign citizens" or "freemen on the land" attempted to argue that they were not subject to U.K. law, including its tax laws. The individuals in this movement believed that they were exempt from paying taxes because they were not "subjects" of the British Crown or citizens of the United Kingdom. They also invoked legal theories based on the belief that common law, rather than statutory law, governed their actions.

In response, the U.K. courts rejected these claims, reinforcing the idea that tax obligations are a legal and moral responsibility for all citizens. The courts consistently ruled that individuals cannot opt out of taxes based on personal beliefs or pseudolegal theories. The U.K. government's stance was clear: tax resistance movements based on freemen-like ideologies have no legal standing, and those who refuse to pay taxes face legal penalties. The failure of these ideologies in the U.K. courts reflects the broader global rejection of these claims, which are often seen as attempts to evade the law rather than legitimate challenges to government authority.

In Australia, similar legal battles have taken place, with freemen-like movements emerging in the early 2000s. These movements, which draw heavily from sovereignty and tax resistance ideologies, often argue that individuals are not legally required to pay taxes. They claim that taxation is a voluntary system and that individuals can choose to reject it based on personal sovereignty beliefs.

Like their counterparts in the U.S., Canada, and the U.K., Australian tax resisters have faced legal repercussions for their actions.

In one high-profile case, an Australian man who had refused to pay taxes based on sovereign citizen arguments was taken to court by the Australian Tax Office (ATO). The individual argued that he was not a "taxpayer" under Australian law and therefore had no obligation to pay taxes. However, the Australian courts rejected his arguments, emphasizing that tax laws applied to all citizens and residents of Australia, regardless of their beliefs about sovereignty. The ATO took swift legal action, and the individual faced significant penalties, including fines and potential imprisonment. The case served as a reminder that the Australian legal system, like those in other countries, has little tolerance for the rejection of tax obligations based on pseudolegal ideologies.

While the legal outcomes for individuals who subscribe to freemen-like ideologies are largely predictable, they are nonetheless significant. These legal battles serve as important case studies in understanding how the courts handle challenges to government authority and taxation. In each of these countries, the legal system has consistently upheld the legitimacy of taxes, emphasizing that citizens and residents are legally obligated to pay taxes as part of their duty to society. The rejection of tax resistance arguments, whether based on personal sovereignty or pseudolegal theories, underscores the strength and resilience of legal systems in enforcing compliance with the law.

What stands out in these cases is the consistency with which courts around the world have rejected the claims put forward by freemen and tax resisters. The legal system, in the United States, Canada, the United Kingdom, and Australia, has overwhelmingly supported the view that taxes are not optional and that individuals cannot opt out of their obligations based on personal beliefs or pseudolegal arguments. Judges and legal experts have consistently ruled that tax laws are constitutional and that the government has the right to collect taxes in order to fund public services and maintain societal structures.

Insights from lawyers and judges who have handled these cases reveal that the legal system is not swayed by the arguments put forward by those who resist taxes. In fact, many legal experts view these claims as a form of legal manipulation, aimed at evading responsibility rather than challenging the legitimacy of government authority. Judges who have ruled on these cases often emphasize that tax resistance movements are based on faulty legal reasoning and that such arguments have no merit in the context of established law.

In conclusion, courtroom battles involving freemen-like ideologies have been fought in numerous countries, but the outcomes have consistently reaffirmed the legality of tax systems and government authority. Across the U.S., U.K., Canada, Australia, and other nations, courts have rejected the arguments put forward by tax resisters and freemen-like individuals. Despite the fervent belief in personal sovereignty and the rejection of government control, the legal system has upheld the principles of taxation and governance. These legal battles demonstrate the resilience of legal systems in the face of challenges from sovereignty movements and underscore the importance of complying with the law, regardless of personal beliefs. The global consistency in these rulings serves as a powerful reminder that, despite the appeal of freemen ideologies, the law remains a force that individuals cannot easily escape.

6 Personal and Societal Costs of Tax Resistance

6 Personal and Societal Costs of Tax Resistance

The allure of sovereignty movements, particularly the rejection of taxation, is not without its consequences. While the ideologies driving freemen and tax resistance movements may promise personal liberation and independence from government control, the realities faced by individuals who embrace these beliefs are often far from ideal. Around the world, the stories of those who have tried to reject the tax systems of their respective countries provide a sobering glimpse into the personal and societal costs of such resistance. From financial ruin to legal trouble, the consequences of opting out of societal obligations are felt deeply by those who engage in these movements. Moreover, the broader societal impact is no less significant, as the strain on legal systems and public resources becomes evident. As the global reach of these movements grows, the ripple effects threaten to undermine trust in governments and institutions.

At the individual level, the personal costs of tax resistance can be devastating. One of the most significant impacts faced by those who reject taxes is financial ruin. Tax resistors often find themselves facing substantial fines, penalties, and even prison sentences for their refusal to comply with tax laws. In many cases, these individuals have lost everything: their savings, their homes, and even their livelihoods. Take, for example, the case of a Canadian man who, after refusing to pay taxes based on sovereign citizen arguments, found himself in significant financial distress. Not only did he face severe fines from the Canada Revenue Agency, but he also found himself unable to repay the mounting debt that came with ignoring tax obligations. As the legal battle dragged on, the financial burden became overwhelming. The man eventually lost his home, a poignant reminder of the high stakes involved in rejecting tax systems that are deeply ingrained in the fabric of society.

Similarly, in the United States, there are numerous stories of individuals who have gone down the path of tax resistance, only to find themselves facing significant personal consequences. One high-profile case involved a man from Ohio who, for years, claimed that he was exempt from paying taxes because he was a "sovereign citizen" who had not consented to the authority of the U.S. government. His beliefs led him to refuse filing tax returns and paying taxes. However, the IRS did not accept his claims, and over time, he accrued substantial penalties and interest on his unpaid taxes. In the end, the man was convicted of tax evasion and sentenced to prison, while his financial situation deteriorated to the point where he was left with little more than a mountain of debt. This story illustrates how the rejection of tax obligations based on pseudolegal theories can result in severe consequences, leaving individuals financially ruined and legally exposed.

The strain on legal systems and public resources is another significant consequence of tax resistance movements. Governments around the world allocate considerable resources to deal with individuals who refuse to pay taxes. The process of tracking down tax resistors, investigating their claims, and enforcing penalties takes up valuable time and resources. These legal battles are costly, both in terms of money and manpower. For example, in the United States, the IRS spends millions of dollars annually in its efforts to combat tax evasion and prosecute those who refuse to pay taxes. In Canada, the Canada Revenue Agency dedicates a large portion of its budget to investigating tax resistance cases, many of which involve individuals who subscribe to freemen ideologies. These resources could otherwise be used for public services or more pressing government needs. The personal cost of tax resistance, then, extends far beyond the individual and affects society as a whole.

The legal system itself is often overwhelmed by the volume of cases involving freemen-like ideologies. Courts in countries such as the

U.S., Canada, the U.K., and Australia are tasked with addressing cases in which individuals argue that they are not subject to taxation, based on personal beliefs or pseudolegal theories. These cases clog the judicial system, causing delays in the resolution of other important legal matters. For instance, in the United Kingdom, the proliferation of sovereign citizen cases has created a backlog in courts, leading to delays for other individuals who are seeking justice. These cases require extensive legal resources, including the time and effort of judges, lawyers, and law enforcement officials. The effect on the judicial system is far-reaching, as the courts are forced to devote significant attention to cases that ultimately do not present legitimate legal arguments.

The societal costs of tax resistance movements extend beyond the legal and financial ramifications for individuals. One of the most profound impacts is the erosion of trust in governments and institutions. Freemen ideologies often rely on the belief that governments are illegitimate and that individuals can exist outside of the legal system. These beliefs, when propagated on a large scale, contribute to a growing mistrust of government institutions and the rule of law. As more individuals reject taxes and other legal obligations based on these ideologies, the legitimacy of governmental authority begins to be questioned. The more widespread these beliefs become, the more fragile the public's trust in government becomes.

In countries where freemen-like movements gain traction, the consequences can be particularly damaging to the social fabric. If large numbers of people begin to believe that they are exempt from taxation or legal obligations, the tax base, which is essential for funding public services such as healthcare, education, and infrastructure, may shrink. This creates a ripple effect, as the loss of tax revenue leads to cutbacks in public services, which can harm the very communities that rely on them. For example, in the U.S., where tax resistors have been known to argue against paying income taxes, the loss of tax revenue has contributed to budgetary shortfalls at the local and state levels. As a result, governments may be forced to reduce funding for essential services, which disproportionately impacts the most vulnerable members of society.

Globally, the rise of freemen-like ideologies poses a threat to the cohesion of societies. The belief in personal sovereignty and the rejection of government control can lead to fragmentation within societies, as individuals withdraw from collective obligations and responsibilities. When large numbers of people opt out of the tax system, it undermines the principles of social contract theory that underpin modern democracies. The social contract is the idea that individuals agree to be governed in exchange for the protection of their rights and the provision of public goods. When individuals begin to reject this contract, the fabric of society becomes less cohesive, and the collective responsibility that binds communities together begins to erode.

The rise of social media and online forums has played a significant role in the spread of freemen ideologies and tax resistance movements. These platforms have allowed individuals to connect with like-minded people from around the world, sharing ideas and strategies for resisting government authority. While the internet has given voice to these movements, it has also allowed them to spread misinformation and pseudolegal arguments that can have dangerous consequences. The ease with which these ideas are shared online means that more individuals are exposed to the rhetoric of tax resistance and personal sovereignty, which can lead them down a path of legal and financial trouble.

In conclusion, the personal and societal costs of tax resistance are significant. While the beliefs driving freemen and tax resistance movements may appear appealing to some, the consequences are far-reaching and often destructive. For individuals, the financial costs can be devastating, leading to fines, penalties, and even imprisonment. The legal systems in countries around the world bear the strain of these movements, with tax resistors tying up valuable resources in their efforts to evade the law. Moreover, the broader societal impact is undeniable, as these movements undermine trust in governments and institutions and threaten the stability of social systems. The global spread of freemen ideologies and tax resistance movements, fueled by social media and online forums, only adds to the complexity of the issue. As these movements continue to grow, the costs to both individuals and society will only increase, highlighting the dangers of rejecting the established legal and tax systems that bind communities together.

7 Risks of Pseudolegal Beliefs in a Global Context

7 Risks of Pseudolegal Beliefs in a Global Context

In today's interconnected world, misinformation spreads at an alarming pace. The rise of pseudolegal ideologies like those embraced by freemen movements has taken advantage of this global connectivity. While the core beliefs behind these movements may vary slightly across countries, the fundamental tenets remain largely the same: rejecting the legitimacy of state authority, particularly in areas like taxation and law enforcement. These ideologies have found fertile ground in a variety of legal systems, from the United States to Australia, from Canada to the U.K., and even in parts of Europe and beyond. What started as localized movements in certain regions has now morphed into a global phenomenon, aided by social media platforms and online forums. The spread of misinformation and the adaptation of these beliefs to fit different legal frameworks pose significant risks not only to individuals who embrace them but to the stability of societies worldwide.

One of the primary ways pseudolegal beliefs have spread internationally is through online platforms. The internet has allowed individuals from across the globe to access and exchange ideas quickly, making it easier for freemen-like ideologies to gain traction. Forums and social media groups dedicated to "sovereign citizen" beliefs and tax resistance have become echo chambers where individuals reinforce one another's misconceptions and beliefs. A simple search online can lead someone down a rabbit hole of pseudolegal arguments, from the misinterpretation of maritime law to the false notion of "freedom from government." These beliefs can be incredibly appealing because they offer the promise of personal autonomy and financial freedom, free from the control of governments. However, the misinformation shared in these online spaces often lacks any legal or factual grounding.

As these ideas spread, they also adapt to the legal systems in which they are propagated. For example, in countries like the United States and Canada, where freemen-like ideologies have a strong presence, the belief that individuals can opt out of paying taxes or refuse to comply with government regulations is widespread. The strategies used by freemen to avoid taxation or legal obligations often center around the use of pseudolegal documents, such as fictitious declarations of sovereignty, and the manipulation of legal language to create the illusion of legality. In the United States, this can include the filing of paperwork claiming that one is not subject to the jurisdiction of the government, while in Canada, individuals may attempt to use similar strategies, often invoking maritime law or other fringe theories that have no basis in Canadian law.

But these tactics are not just limited to North America. In countries like the U.K., Australia, and parts of Europe, freemen-like ideologies have also gained a foothold, and the local legal systems are struggling to keep up. In the U.K., for example, the courts have been flooded with cases involving individuals who refuse to recognize the authority of the state, using arguments that are rooted in pseudolegal beliefs. These arguments often revolve around the idea that individuals can opt out of the system by invoking certain legal or philosophical concepts, such as the Magna Carta or other historical documents, despite the fact that these documents are no longer legally relevant in most modern jurisdictions. The rise of freemen-like ideologies in these countries has led to an increase in legal challenges and, in some cases, prolonged court battles that drain resources and undermine the legal system's ability to function efficiently.

The consequences of embracing pseudolegal beliefs can be severe, both for individuals and society at large. Those who attempt to use freemen-like arguments in court often find that they are met with resistance from the legal system. In many cases, the courts will dismiss these arguments outright, and the individuals involved are left facing escalating penalties and fines. In some instances, these individuals have been subjected to imprisonment for failing to pay taxes or refusing to comply with legal orders. The case of a man in Australia, who attempted to claim that he was not subject to Australian law, serves as a poignant example of the consequences of relying on pseudolegal beliefs. After years of challenging government authorities and refusing to pay taxes, the man eventually found himself in legal and financial ruin. The penalties accumulated over time were substantial, and his efforts to evade the law only led to further punishment. This is a common theme among those who embrace these ideologies: their belief in personal sovereignty ultimately results in financial and legal hardships that could have been avoided by following the law.

These failed strategies and the escalating penalties that result from them highlight the dangers of adopting pseudolegal beliefs. While the initial allure of sovereignty movements may seem appealing, the reality is that individuals who follow these ideologies often find themselves caught in a web of legal challenges that they are ill-prepared to navigate. As more people buy into these ideas, they face an uphill battle against a legal system that is designed to uphold the rule of law. The system is not flexible enough to accommodate the notion of individual sovereignty, and courts are quick to reject pseudolegal arguments, particularly when they fail to recognize the authority of the state.

The societal impact of these movements extends beyond the individual. When large numbers of people begin to reject the law and attempt to operate outside of the legal framework, the stability of society is threatened. Governments rely on a functioning legal system to maintain order, ensure justice, and provide for the welfare of their citizens. When individuals opt out of this system, it creates a void that can lead to chaos and disorder. Freemen-like movements pose a direct challenge to the concept of social contract theory, which holds that individuals have an obligation to obey the laws of the state in exchange for protection and the provision of public goods. When individuals reject this social contract, the foundations of societal order begin to erode, leading to a breakdown in trust and a weakening of the institutions that underpin modern governance.

Moreover, as freemen-like ideologies spread internationally, they begin to have a global impact. The rise of online forums and social media groups has created an environment in which misinformation can easily cross borders and influence individuals in different parts of the world. This global spread of pseudolegal beliefs presents a challenge for governments and legal systems, as they must contend with a growing number of individuals who are unwilling to comply with the law. The rise of these ideologies can also lead to an increase in anti-government sentiment, as individuals begin to question the legitimacy of their governments and institutions. This erosion of trust in authority can have serious consequences, as it can lead to widespread disillusionment with the political system and undermine the effectiveness of government policies.

In conclusion, the risks posed by pseudolegal beliefs are far-reaching and significant. While the appeal of sovereignty movements may be strong, the consequences of embracing these ideologies are often dire. Individuals who reject the legal system based on pseudolegal arguments frequently face escalating penalties, legal battles, and financial ruin. The global spread of these beliefs, aided by social media and online forums, threatens to destabilize societies and undermine trust in governments and institutions. As more people are drawn into the web of misinformation, the risks posed by these movements will continue to grow, making it imperative for legal systems and governments around the world to address these challenges. The promotion of accurate legal information and the debunking of pseudolegal arguments will be crucial in mitigating the impact of these movements and ensuring that societies remain stable and orderly.

8 Debunking Global Freemen Myths

8 Debunking Global Freemen Myths

The spread of freemen-like ideologies, with their promises of freedom from taxation and the rejection of governmental authority, has sparked numerous legal and societal debates across the world. While the ideas may seem appealing to some, they are deeply flawed have no basis in law. In this chapter, we will take a closer look at some of the most common myths propagated by freemen movements and provide clear, fact-based explanations of why these beliefs are incorrect. By debunking these myths, we hope to equip individuals with the knowledge to avoid falling prey to misinformation and provide clarity on their legal rights and obligations.

The first and perhaps most prominent myth embraced by freemen-like groups is the claim that individuals can somehow "opt out" of the tax system or any legal system simply by declaring themselves sovereign. This idea is rooted in the belief that governments only have jurisdiction over those who consent to be governed, and that one can free themselves from legal obligations through the declaration of independence. The reality, however, is that governments derive their authority from a variety of sources, including constitutions, laws, and treaties, which apply to all citizens, regardless of whether or not they consent to them. These claims are rooted in the idea of "natural law," which asserts that certain rights exist independent of government and that individuals can assert these rights to reject governmental authority. However, natural law as it is used by freemen-like groups is not legally recognized in any modern legal system.

Across different legal contexts, the idea that individuals can "opt out" of the law simply by making a declaration is not only flawed but dangerous. Whether operating under common law, civil law, or mixed legal systems, the laws governing individuals are clear and binding. In common law countries like the United States, Canada, and the U.K., the legal system is based on the principle of stare decisis, or the idea that past legal decisions should guide current rulings. This system, built on centuries of legal precedent, does not allow for individuals to simply declare themselves outside the law by invoking pseudolegal arguments. The courts in these countries are well-equipped to dismiss such claims, as they have no grounding in real legal principles. The idea of a "sovereign citizen" rejecting government authority has been thoroughly tested in the courts, and the overwhelming legal consensus is that individuals cannot simply remove themselves from the legal system.

In civil law countries, such as those in much of Europe and Latin America, the legal systems operate under codified statutes that are designed to be clear and comprehensive. These legal systems, which have their roots in Roman law, do not recognize the concept of individual sovereignty in the way that freemen-like ideologies suggest. Civil law systems operate on the principle that laws are created by legislatures and must be followed by all citizens, regardless of personal belief or declaration. Individuals in civil law countries do not have the option to opt out of taxes or reject legal obligations simply by invoking a pseudolegal argument. The legal framework is designed to ensure that all citizens are treated equally under the law, and any attempt to circumvent this system is likely to result in legal penalties.

In mixed legal systems, such as those found in countries like South Africa or Japan, elements of both common law and civil law may apply, but the principle remains the same: legal obligations cannot be avoided by making a personal declaration of sovereignty. In these countries, as in others, the rule of law applies to all citizens, regardless of personal beliefs or declarations. Freemen-like claims are not recognized by the legal systems in these countries, and those who attempt to use such arguments in court will quickly find that their claims are dismissed as baseless.

Beyond the legal realm, freemen-like ideologies often rely on a series of pseudolegal myths about taxation. One of the most common myths is that taxation is somehow illegal or unconstitutional. This claim is often based on a misinterpretation of constitutional principles or the deliberate distortion of legal language. In the United States, for example, freemen-like groups often point to the 16th Amendment, which allows for the federal income tax, and claim that it was never properly ratified. However, this claim has been thoroughly debunked by legal scholars and courts, and it has no basis in fact. The 16th Amendment has been legally recognized and upheld by the U.S. Supreme

Court, and taxation remains a fundamental part of the U.S. legal system.

Similar misconceptions about taxation exist in other countries as well. In the U.K., freemen-like groups often argue that they are not subject to tax laws because they have not given their consent to be governed. However, this argument is based on a fundamental misunderstanding of the nature of taxation and the social contract. Taxation is not about individual consent; it is a legal obligation that is necessary to fund the functioning of government and public services. The notion that individuals can simply reject this obligation is a myth that has no grounding in reality. Tax laws in the U.K. are clear and have been upheld by the courts for centuries.

In countries like Canada and Australia, freemen-like groups often invoke similar arguments, claiming that they are not subject to taxation or government authority because they are not "citizens" in the legal sense. These claims are equally false and have been rejected by the courts in both countries. The legal concept of citizenship is defined by law, and individuals are subject to the legal obligations of their country, including the payment of taxes, whether they personally agree with them or not.

One of the most dangerous aspects of the freemen movement is the spread of misinformation. As these beliefs have spread across the globe, they have been amplified by social media and online forums. These platforms provide a space for individuals to share their beliefs and experiences, but they also allow misinformation to thrive unchecked. Social media platforms are rife with videos, posts, and articles that perpetuate pseudolegal arguments and distortions of the law. These platforms allow people to reinforce their own beliefs, no matter how far-fetched they may be, and discourage independent research into the validity of these claims.

The problem with social media is that it creates echo chambers, where individuals can surround themselves with people who share their misconceptions and reinforce one another's beliefs. This feedback loop makes it difficult for individuals to engage with opposing viewpoints or to critically evaluate the information they are being fed.

Misinformation spreads quickly, and the more people who see these claims, the more likely they are to believe them, regardless of how untrue or legally unsound they are. This is particularly troubling when it comes to matters as serious as taxation and legal obligations, where misinformation can have real-world consequences.

What makes this even more troubling is that social media platforms often lack the necessary mechanisms to properly fact-check and debunk these myths. While some platforms have begun to take steps to combat misinformation, many pseudolegal arguments still slip through the cracks. This lack of oversight allows pseudolegal myths to flourish and be propagated globally. As a result, more and more people are drawn into the freemen-like ideologies, often without understanding the full implications of their beliefs.

In the face of these challenges, it is essential for individuals to be able to recognize and counter misinformation. This starts with understanding the basic principles of law and taxation in their respective countries. By educating themselves about the legal systems they live under, people can better discern fact from fiction and avoid falling victim to pseudolegal claims. It is also important to seek out reliable sources of information, such as legal experts, government websites, and reputable news outlets, to counter the misinformation they may encounter online. Finally, individuals should engage with opposing viewpoints and question the sources of the information they come across. By doing so, they can break free from the echo chambers of misinformation and develop a more accurate understanding of the world around them.

In conclusion, the myths perpetuated by freemen-like movements are not only false but also dangerous. These pseudolegal arguments have no basis in law and can lead individuals down a path of legal and financial ruin. As these beliefs continue to spread through social media and online platforms, it is more important than ever for individuals to educate themselves and engage critically with the information they encounter. By debunking these myths and understanding the true nature of law and taxation, individuals can protect themselves from the consequences of misinformation and ensure that they are living within the legal frameworks of their respective countries.

9 Rebuilding Trust and Advocacy Worldwide

9 Rebuilding Trust and Advocacy Worldwide

Across the globe, there is an ongoing struggle between individuals and governments, with many feeling disconnected from the institutions that are supposed to serve them. This disconnection often fosters a sense of injustice, and some turn to pseudolegal movements as an alternative way of addressing their grievances. However, the reality is that these movements are not a solution to the issues people face. Instead, they often lead to further problems, including legal entanglements, financial ruin, and the erosion of trust in legitimate systems. In this chapter, we will explore how individuals can address their grievances in ethical and legal ways, how civic engagement can create meaningful change within any system, and how we can encourage informed global citizenship to counter the influence of pseudolegal myths.

The first step in rebuilding trust is understanding that grievances with government systems are not inherently unjust or unique. Governments, by their nature, are complex and often operate under systems that are difficult to navigate. It's not uncommon for individuals to feel that they are being treated unfairly, especially when dealing with bureaucratic systems that seem impersonal or even corrupt. In many cases, these grievances can be legitimate. However, turning to pseudolegal myths and conspiracy theories only prevents the possibility of real change and perpetuates division. Instead, addressing grievances through legal, ethical, and peaceful means can lead to positive outcomes, while ensuring that individuals remain within the framework of the law.

In every country, there are ethical and legal ways to address grievances with the government. Whether the issue is high taxation, unfair regulations, or a lack of transparency, there are channels through which people can make their voices heard. These channels differ from country to country, but they all share the common goal of ensuring that citizens can participate in shaping the policies and laws that govern them. The key is understanding the legitimate avenues for change and how individuals can navigate them.

One of the most powerful ways to address grievances is through formal petitions and advocacy. In many countries, citizens have the right to petition their government, whether through local or national channels. Petitions can be an effective way to bring attention to an issue, rally support, and encourage change. In democratic societies, petitions often serve as a starting point for policy discussions, while in authoritarian regimes, they can be a method of peaceful protest and a tool for public awareness.

Another crucial tool for addressing grievances is through the court system. Legal challenges against government actions or policies are an essential part of maintaining the rule of law. The courts provide a mechanism for individuals to contest government actions that they believe are unjust or unconstitutional. While the legal system may not always provide a perfect solution, it is an important safeguard for protecting citizens' rights and ensuring that governments are held accountable for their actions. In some countries, citizens can bring class-action lawsuits against government entities or corporations, allowing them to address issues that affect entire communities or populations. By using the legal system to address grievances, individuals can promote a culture of justice and fairness within their countries.

In many nations, there are also opportunities for people to participate in the political process. Voting, running for office, or engaging in public debate are all valid ways to influence government decisions. Civic engagement is a cornerstone of democracy, and participating in the electoral process helps ensure that government policies reflect the will of the people. When people choose to engage with the political system through voting or activism, they are helping to shape a future that aligns with their values and needs. Advocacy groups, community organizing, and public demonstrations are also powerful ways for individuals to address grievances and push for change, ensuring that their voices are heard in a meaningful way.

An essential aspect of rebuilding trust in governmental systems is recognizing the role of public servants. While governments can sometimes feel distant or ineffective, public servants — the individuals who work within these systems — are often motivated by a desire to improve the public good. In many cases, bureaucrats, elected officials, and other government employees are working hard to address the needs of their constituents, even if it doesn't always feel like it. By fostering a spirit of cooperation and understanding between the public and government officials, trust can begin to be rebuilt. Engaging with public servants through town halls, constituent services, and community meetings can provide a direct line of communication and help break down barriers between individuals and the government.

One of the most profound and lasting ways to rebuild trust is through education. Civic education empowers citizens with the knowledge and skills needed to navigate complex legal and political systems. When individuals are educated about their rights and responsibilities, they are better equipped to hold their governments accountable. This education is especially important when it comes to understanding the legal systems within each country. By learning about the laws that govern taxation, property rights, and civil liberties, individuals can make more informed decisions and resist the influence of pseudolegal myths that have no basis in fact.

Education also plays a key role in encouraging people to think critically about the information they encounter. In the age of social media and online forums, misinformation spreads rapidly. Many of the pseudolegal myths promoted by freemen-like movements are fueled by a lack of understanding and critical thinking. Social media platforms are rife with sensationalized claims about taxation and the nature of government, and these falsehoods can be particularly convincing to those who are unfamiliar with the legal system. However, by promoting critical thinking and encouraging people to verify the information they come across, we can counter the spread of misinformation and create a more informed citizenry.

Civic engagement and public participation are crucial in shaping the systems we live under. In order to create positive change, it is essential for individuals to take ownership of their rights and responsibilities. Advocacy, whether through petitions, the legal system, or political participation, is a powerful tool for ensuring that government decisions reflect the needs and desires of the people. However, it is just as important for individuals to be vigilant about the information they consume and share. By engaging with legitimate sources and thinking critically about the information they encounter, individuals can resist the influence of pseudolegal movements and contribute to a more informed and democratic society.

In addition to educating individuals, we must also focus on reforming the systems themselves. Governments, like any institution, are not perfect. There are areas where inefficiencies, corruption, and abuses of power exist. Addressing these issues through systemic reforms is essential for rebuilding trust. This could involve increasing transparency in government dealings, improving the accessibility of legal processes, or enacting reforms to ensure that the needs of marginalized groups are better addressed. Structural reforms that focus on accountability and fairness are key to creating a government that people can trust and rely on.

The final piece in the puzzle of rebuilding trust is collective action. While individual advocacy is crucial, change is most effective when it is driven by a broad base of support. Social movements, community organizing, and grassroots campaigns can amplify the voices of those who are seeking to make change.

When individuals come together and work toward a common goal, they can create a ripple effect that transforms society. By building alliances, sharing knowledge, and organizing efforts, individuals can help rebuild trust in governmental systems and work toward a more just and equitable world.

In conclusion, rebuilding trust in government and advocating for positive change requires a combination of education, civic engagement, and systemic reform. By addressing grievances through ethical and legal channels, participating in the political process, and fostering critical thinking, individuals can contribute to the creation of a society that is more transparent, accountable, and just. The global community must work together to resist the pull of pseudolegal myths and misinformation, and instead focus on creating a future where citizens have the knowledge, tools, and resources to engage with their governments in meaningful ways. By fostering informed global citizenship, we can begin to rebuild trust in systems that serve the common good, ensuring that these systems are not only effective but also reflective of the values and needs of all people.

Conclusion A Universal Call for Critical Thinking

Conclusion A Universal Call for Critical Thinking

The global freemen movement, though seemingly appealing to those disillusioned with governmental structures, has had a profound impact across borders. From the streets of North America to the countrysides of Europe and the far reaches of Oceania, the freemen ideologies have captured the imaginations of many. Yet, despite their widespread presence, these movements have often failed to offer any real solutions to the problems they purport to address. Instead, they have caused individuals to fall into legal traps, face financial ruin, and foster distrust in the very systems designed to protect them. As we wrap up our exploration of the freemen movement, it is clear that the lessons learned from this phenomenon are universal: trust in the system is not built through rejection, but through understanding and thoughtful engagement.

Throughout this book, we've seen how the freemen movement, despite its variations, operates on a foundation of misinformation and pseudolegal arguments that have been tested and disproven time and time again. These ideologies, whether born out of frustration with taxes, the perceived overreach of governments, or a distrust of authority, are ultimately built on false premises. What begins as a well-meaning attempt to reclaim personal sovereignty or financial freedom often spirals into chaos, as individuals are led to believe that they can opt out of laws, taxes, and legal obligations simply by invoking terms and legal myths that have no basis in reality.

The truth is, real change comes not from rejecting systems outright, but from understanding them and working within them. The key to effective change, whether at the personal, local, or global level, lies in understanding the laws and systems that govern us and participating thoughtfully and actively in the process. Rather than turning away from the system, we must engage with it in a way that is informed, legal, and ethical. When we are equipped with knowledge, critical thinking, and a willingness to work within the framework of the law, we are not only protecting ourselves from harm, but we are also creating the conditions for meaningful and lasting change.

In the end, critical thinking is the antidote to misinformation. It is easy to be swept up in the allure of simplified solutions or to fall prey to the comfort of easy answers that are fed to us through social media, online forums, or charismatic leaders. But the real power lies in our ability to question, to research, and to understand the complex world around us. As we've seen, the freemen movement's claims are based on misconceptions and a lack of understanding of legal systems. When we take the time to educate ourselves, to ask the hard questions, and to think critically about the information we encounter, we arm ourselves with the tools to resist the spread of false ideologies.

A significant part of rebuilding trust in our global systems lies in cultivating this mindset of critical engagement. The systems we live under, while imperfect, were not created in vain. In every country, there are legitimate ways to address grievances, protest unjust actions, and seek reform. These channels exist because systems of governance, though flawed, are built to evolve and respond to the needs of the people. Change is possible, but only when we engage with these systems thoughtfully, using the tools available to us in ways that are both legal and ethical.

As we conclude this journey through the freemen movement and the importance of critical thinking, I urge you to take these lessons to heart. Whether you are struggling with your own frustrations regarding taxes, government actions, or the perception of a lack of justice, remember that rejecting the system will not bring you peace or solutions. Understanding it, questioning it, and engaging with it in informed, legal ways is the true path to progress. This is not just a call for individuals to think critically—it is a call for global citizenship, where each of us takes responsibility for our role in shaping a fairer, more just world.

Now, more than ever, we must be vigilant in resisting misinformation and pseudolegal ideologies. The global freemen movement has shown us the dangers of believing in easy answers, but it has also provided an opportunity to reflect on the value of knowledge, understanding, and engagement. By continuing to educate ourselves, to ask questions, and to challenge false narratives, we can protect ourselves and others from falling into the traps that these movements set. More importantly, by actively participating in our societies—whether through lawful protest, civic engagement, or simply being informed—we can create the positive changes we seek.

So, let this be a call to action for us all. We are not bound by the myths of pseudolegal beliefs, but by the power of knowledge, the strength of our legal systems, and the potential for meaningful change when we work within the systems that exist. True freedom comes not from avoiding our responsibilities, but from fully understanding them and using them to create a better future for ourselves and the world around us.

RP Macleod

www.ingramcontent.com/pod-product-compliance
Lightning Source LLC
Chambersburg PA
CBHW071416220526
45469CB00004B/1298